LEAVING THE LADIES

Sinéad McCoole

LEAVING THE LADIES

ARLEN
HOUSE

Leaving the Ladies

is published in 2019 by
ARLEN HOUSE
42 Grange Abbey Road
Baldoyle
Dublin 13
Ireland
Phone: 353 86 8360236
Email: arlenhouse@gmail.com
arlenhouse.blogspot.com

ISBN 978–1–85132–219–0, paperback

International distribution
SYRACUSE UNIVERSITY PRESS
621 Skytop Road, Suite 110
Syracuse
New York 13244–5290
USA
Phone: 315–443–5534/Fax: 315–443–5545
Email: supress@syr.edu
www.syracuseuniversitypress.syr.edu

Typesetting by Arlen House

Front cover: 'Hibernia' by Lily Williams, 1916 (pastel on paper)
is reproduced courtesy of The O'Brien Collection
Photography by Michael Tropea

Back cover painting of Dr Kathleen Lynn by Lily Williams (1919)
is reproduced courtesy of the Irish Labour History Society

Contents

for my mother
Barbara Folan McCoole

This play is based on an actual event which took place on 11 December 1917, in the bathroom beside the Round Room in the Mansion House; a place where many of the key political gatherings occurred.

This was no chance meeting of a group of ladies in the lavatory; instead it was an organised and minuted meeting of Women Delegates to the All Ireland Conference. This meeting is recorded in a minute book which is now in the National Library of Ireland [*Hanna Sheehy Skeffington Papers, MS 21,194 (47)*].

This meeting was attended by some of the most important and influential women of the day: members of organisations such as Cumann na mBan, the Irish Women Workers' Union and the Irish Citizen Army – some of whom had fought in the Easter Rising the previous year.

This dramatised version of a real event is set against the backdrop of the final stage of agitation by the 'Votes for Women' campaigners who were trying to attain full suffrage as the Representation of the People bill was being drafted.

CAST

Constance de Markievicz, *age 49*

Rosamond Jacob, *age 29*

Dulcibella Barton, *age 37*

Mary Perolz, *age 43*

Margaret 'Loo' Kennedy, *age 25*

Alice Ginnell, *age 34*

Dr Kathleen Lynn, *age 43*

Effie Kelly, *age 18*

Flora Allsopp, *age 34*

Violet Tait, *age 25*

Male and female hecklers

CONSTANCE DE MARKIEVICZ was known by her close friends as Con and by most as Madame Markievicz. She had been released from prison in England some six months before this meeting. In 1916 she had been vice commander in St Stephen's Green and the College of Surgeons. She was sentenced to death, but the charge was commuted because she was a woman. A painter, she had studied in Paris, where she met Casimir Dunin de Markievicz, a member of the Polish nobility. They were now separated, he was fighting in Europe. Their daughter Maeve had been brought up by Con's mother in Sligo since she was an infant.

ROSAMOND JACOB, a Quaker from Waterford, was active in the Gaelic League and the organisation of the Irish Women's Francise League, as well as being a member of Cumann na mBan. She was a committed Sinn Féiner, who made it well-known in her native town that she supported the Rising. She and her brother Tom, her only surviving sibling, joined several political organisations. They founded their own branch of Sinn Féin in 1905. Rosamond left school at 16; she attended the local technical school where she undertook jewellery making. She was still living in Waterford with her mother Henrietta when she attended this meeting. She was an inspiring novelist.

DULCIBELLA BARTON, Da to her friends, was one of the 'Big House' Irish. At the time of this meeting she was the unmarried sister living in the homeplace – Glendalough House, Annamoe, County Wicklow – which had been expanded in size in the 1880s to accommodate her Childers cousins who came to live there when their parents died. Her three brothers had joined the British Army at the start of the Great War; Robert, known as Bob, was on home duty. They shared an interest in Irish nationalist politics. In 1917 Dulcibella founded a Sinn Féin club on the family farm and one in nearby Laragh. In contrast, her only surviving sister, Margaret, had moved to England and had little interest in Ireland and its politics.

MARY PEROLZ was, in her own words, 'into everything'. She had joined every nationalist organisation and was an active worker in Liberty Hall. In the run-up to the Rising she was going to take a position in Singers as assistant accountant, but James Connolly told her to turn it down – there would be plenty of work for her after the Rising. Her outspoken ways landed her in prison and she was proud that she was one of the women imprisoned the longest, despite the fact that she had not been in the actual fight. She had been sent out of the city as a trusted courier before the fight began.

MARGARET AGNES KENNEDY, always known as Loo, was the youngest of five surviving sisters, living at 117 Donore Avenue, South Circular Road, Dublin. The family took in boarders and Margaret engaged in 'home duties'. Active from her teenage years, she was a member of Cumann na mBan and was in the Inghinidhe na hÉireann branch, which was made up of women who had been members of Maud Gonne's Daughters of Ireland founded in 1900. 'Out' in 1916 she was a member of the Marrowbone Lane Garrison and was held for eight days in Kilmainham Gaol.

DR KATHLEEN LYNN had been the Chief Medical Officer of the Irish Citizen Army in the 1916 Rising. The past year had been a difficult time for her, cut off by her family for so publicly bringing attention to 'her politics'. Her father was rector at Ashford Castle, Cong, County Mayo – he could not have been more opposed to those who had been in the Rising. A general practitioner, Kathleen's specialisation was paediatrics. Her relationship with Madeleine ffrench-Mullen was an open secret.

ALICE GINNELL, formerly Alice King of Kilbride, Mullingar, at the age of 19 married a widower, Laurence Ginnell, following the untimely death of his first wife and their child. They were married 15 years but had not had children of their own. In 1915 Alice joined Cumann na mBan in London where they lived because Laurence was working in Westminster as MP for North Westmeath, but in June 1917 they sold their house and returned to Ireland. Her husband had decided to give his alligence to Sinn Féin.

EFFIE KELLY represents the rank and file of the Cumann na mBan organisation. She is committed to their ideals – to a point. Her choice between love and marriage, and her love of and commitment to the movement for independence for Ireland is central to this dramatisation.

FLORA ALLSOPP, a university-educated, well-spoken Dublin woman.

VIOLET TAIT, a university-educated, well-spoken Galway woman.

LEAVING THE LADIES

ACT ONE

Curtain up.

A rally outside the Mansion House, Dawson Street, Dublin.

Two members of the suffrage movement, FLORA ALLSOPP and VIOLET TAIT, are addressing a small crowd. There are 2 male and 2 female HECKLERS.

MUSIC: *Men singing an anti-suffrage chant. Drum beating.*

FLORA ALLSOPP (*using megaphone*): Votes for women! Universal suffrage! The extension of the vote to all adults!

VIOLET TAIT: Without distinction to race! Or sex! Or belief!

MALE HECKLER I: Hey ladies, don't you read the papers! Women *are* getting the vote!

FLORA ALLSOPP: Votes for *all* women and men!

MALE HECKLER II: Youse are never happy! Like an organ grinder you lot are always complaining and cribbing.

Sound of an organ grinder making music in the background.

FLORA ALLSOPP (*shouting*): The House of Lords will shortly pass the Representation of the People bill.

MALE HECKLER I: *Not* my people, luv! Home Rule is gone! Up Sinn Féin! Sinn Féin Abu!

FLORA ALLSOPP: Sir, please, we are a peaceful gathering. A sisterhood of united people seeking a part in parliament.

MALE HECKLER I: The United Kingdom is being broken up! Three cheers for the returned prisoners! The Sinn Féiners are out! Up the Republic!

Inaudible jeers and wolf whistles.

MALE HECKLER II: Women are unfit for public life!

FLORA ALLSOPP (*using a megaphone*): Sir, we ask is public life fit for women? We need women in parliament, in government. We still have to fight for votes for all women!

MALE HECKLER I: You're getting that! What are you fighting about?

FLORA ALLSOPP (*not using megaphone*): I beg your pardon, sir, the Represention of the People bill offers limited franchise. Ladies, can I ask you, will you support our cause?

FEMALE HECKLER I (*Sound of scuffling, pushing and shoving*): Arragh? Jeysus. Yer wasting your time talking to us. Ye're in the wrong part of town. Off up to the university with ye.

FLORA ALLSOPP (*speaking directly to the woman*): Indeed ladies who are attending the university make up much of our league's membership. Madame, we welcome members who have not attended university.

FEMALE HECKLER II: Youse have no idea! We need cheap rent ... food ... jobs! I've had enough of ye, too much time with nothing to do. I'll wager you never scrubbed a floor! You're welcome to come to my university. Study my life! Huh! (*Laughter*).

FLORA ALLSOPP: Ladies, may I introduce Miss Tait, a member of the Connacht Women's Franchise League who has joined me today.

VIOLET TAIT (*in a low voice*): Thank you, Flora. (*Louder*). I have come from Galway to ask the people of Dublin to make sure to encourage your menfolk ... um ... including members of new organisations who are gathering here today – welcome gentlemen – to make sure you know that ladies want to be active participants in public life, to do practical things that affect all our lives ... having a say in the law, decision making ...

SOME FEMALE VOICES IN THE CROWD: Hear! Hear!

VIOLET TAIT: Are you over 30, madame?

FEMALE HECKLER II: Why would a woman admit her age?

Wolf whistle.

MALE HECKLER II: You must be sweet sixteen, I'd say. Never been kissed.

FEMALE HECKLER II: Get off me, ye stinkin' bowsie. You porter breath! I'm old enough to be your mother!

FLORA ALLSOPP: Violet, Miss Tait, has very kindly travelled hours to be here. She is one of our foot soldiers fighting our just cause. Can you tell people gathered here today what we can do?

VIOLET TAIT: Letter writing, handing out leaflets, talking to friends and family are all ways to spread the message.

MALE HECKLER I: No babbies to mind, no husbands to feed! I'm off!

VIOLET TAIT: ... Umm ... what was I saying ... *(with megaphone)* ... it is proposed that women over thirty and who are on the rates register ...

FLORA ALLSOPP: Everybody knows that we cannot stop at those who own property. Or at the limit of thirty years of age!

VIOLET TAIT: I'll be postively middle aged before we get the vote *(giggles)*. We need to keep lobbying! We have to add a million or two more to the number of women voters who can put MPs in Westminster!

MALE HECKLER I: We won't need to go to Westminster! Up Eamon de Valera! Up Count Plunkett!

DR KATHLEEN LYNN *enters the crowd.*

DR LYNN *(raised voice)*: Take our leaflet! Please take our leaflet! The leaders of the Rising proclaimed equality for women. The Proclamation was addressed to men and women – equally. A Republic will have equal rights for all its citizens.

FLORA ALLSOPP *(with megaphone)*: Dr Lynn, I welcome you to come up to our stand. Have you not been for many years a member of the suffrage movement? You agree with universal suffrage. The extension of the vote to all adults. Surely you agree that the current plan to curb the right to women over thirty who have property is incorrect. Dr Lynn – are you committed to fight for the right to vote for all adults without distinction as to race or social status? Join us. We are open to women of every shade of political opinion … Ladies and gentlemen, I have been a member since the early days when your friend Mrs Sheehy Skeffington went to prison for our cause. I know that you tended the women imprisoned for protesting their right to vote. I would be much obliged if you joined us up here – or failing that to take our leaflet, 'Outlines of a scheme of the interchange of social knowledge among Irish women'.

DR LYNN: Thank you. I will read your literature gladly, but I am on my way to my own meeting. I am now a member of a delegation of women; a group which is working towards a new Ireland when women will walk the corridors of power in parliament – but we don't want it to be Westminster. New voices in politics. New politics.

MALE HECKLER II: Oh no! I've heard enough! Who wants new politics!

VIOLET TAIT (*loud whisper*): Excuse me, Flora. I object to you asking Dr Lynn to join us here on our platform. I am here to represent members of the *non-militant* Connacht Women's Franchise League. We want to obtain parliamentary franchise for women on the same terms as men, but we did not agree with the militants' methods in breaking windows and hunger strikes in prison. And Dr Lynn was part of a revolution not quite a year ago!

Crowd clapping.

VIOLET TAIT (*using a megaphone*): I don't want anything to do with women of violence.

FEMALE HECKLER I: I'm with Madame Markievicz. Wear short skirts and buy a revolver! Ha! Ha!

MALE HECKLER II: Your lot were no better. Smashing windows! Destroying public property! Arson! Home-made bombs! Suffragettes!

VIOLET TAIT: Excuse me, sir! We consider ourselves *suffragists!* We are not with those that did those acts. Many of those suffragettes came to Ireland from England. We don't condone their methods. We are today representing those who advocate non-violent action to get our aim!

MALE HECKLER I: Oh! Good luck with that! I am up for the doctor here. She showed her pluck when she took City Hall last year. Fair dues to her. Not all talk ... I like a woman of action myself!

FEMALE HECKLERS CHANTING:
Convicts and women kindly note *(laughter)*
Are not allowed to have the vote
The difference between the two
I will now indicate to you
When once the harmful man of crime
In Wormwood Scrubs has done his time
He at the poll can have his say.
The harmless women never may.*

* *an actual ditty from this time.*

ACT TWO

The ladies lavatory at the Mansion House – a group of eight mainly middle-aged women – CONSTANCE DE MARKIEVICZ, DULCIBELLA BARTON, ROSAMOND JACOB, LOO KENNEDY, MARY PEROLZ, ALICE GINNELL *with* DR KATHLEEN LYNN *in the chair, and one fictional character,* EFFIE KELLY.

Timid knocking.

MARY (*loud whisper*): It is me, it's Mary. The attendant told me you were all in there! Let me in!

More impatient knocking.

ROSAMOND: I'm coming.

The door opens.

ROSAMOND: Come in. Be quick. The door wasn't locked! We were talking and nobody heard you.

MARY: I am sorry, Rosie.

ROSAMOND (*sharply*): It is Rosamond, Mary. You know that. Or perhaps you should call me Miss Jacob! Why do you need to always draw attention to yourself? We don't want to draw attention to the fact that we have to hold our meeting here.

MARY (*laughing*): I am an activist! I believe in bringing attention to my cause. You're only put out because I got infamous for being put in prison for my part in the Rising! Now everyone knows me, Mary Perolz … (*emphasing*) PER OOOLS …

CONSTANCE (*interrupting*): Stop it you two, bickering like the ne'er-do-wells I met in prison. There is no need to take a role of honour here. We all have shown our loyalty to the Republic. There will be time for Rosamond to take her part. Mary, I take it there is a reason why you are late?

LOO: What's happened now?

MARY: When I got off the tram I knew I was being followed. That same DMP policeman – you know that should stand for DIM-minded people, not Dublin

Metropolitan Police. They think they are undercover, when you just know, you just know, every time by their walk, the look on their faces. So I turned around and said to him straight up. I said … wielding my umbrella … that I knew him. Then he says to me (*mock deep voice*) he says to me … 'stop shaking that weapon, Madame'. I says to him – I am no Madame! 'Begging your pardon, Madame Markievicz'. You know they always think I am you … didn't I fool a whole load of them in Kerry that time … (*laughing*). Heaven help me, I am tall and thin, but there our comparsion ends …

CONSTANCE: Mary, we need to commence this meeting. You do understand how important today is for our cause, for Ireland?

MARY: I surely do. Didn't I wear my tricolour pin that I got at the O'Donovan Rossa's funeral, Lord have mercy on his soul. I am also wearing my Votes for Women badge, the same one that poor Frank Sheehy Skeffington was wearing when he drew his final breath – a feminist, an upholder of liberty until the end! A pacifist killed at the hands of a cold-blooded murderer, a hired assassin, in the uniform of a soldier.

DULCIBELLA (*interrupting*): I don't mean to cut across this exchange … I was never arrested I am glad to say. I would not have endured being in jail, used as I am to open air life … but … we need to get on here. This is a meeting we need to start before they meet in the next room …

LOO: We have no allies in there, now that all the men who led the rebellion last year are dead.

MARY: So many widows because of the actions of great men – just a year cold in their graves. Sure wasn't it Tom Clarke himself who gave me this very pin, this tricolour, that I wear with pride. I did not mean to be late, I did not mean for it to happen, it just did. The policeman asked me about the pin, very aggressively, said he could imprison me. I told him I had been there before and I wasn't afraid. I said, shame on you, an Irishman talking about arresting me for wearing my own country's colours and I showed him me other button saying I should have my vote to elect someone to represent me in parliament. I told him I had me rights. I did! I also said to him, I did, that the great James Connolly, Lord have mercy on his soul, is looking down on him and me, and he had taught me all I know about being confident in me beliefs. I said, looking up at him, standing as tall as I could, until I eyeballed him, I said, you can bring me in. I said, mark my words, young man, you'll see one day we will get our due, our vote, our free country. I turned on my heel and he did not come after me again. I came here as quickly as I could. I had no idea where any of youse were, until the porter said, 'I saw your lot go in there', and I saw he meant the lavatory. I said to him, you're having me on … but he shook his head, he did, and said, 'I have counted seven of them go in and they still have not come out and it was ten minutes ago. I can't go in there, so I think you better go and see for yourself', he laughed then and said, 'they may be powdering their noses or who knows what they're powdering!' (*She laughs, and some of the women laugh as well*).

MARY: Why are youse in here anyway?

DULCIBELLA: Mary, this meeting was called by Con, before the meeting of the nationalist groups who are coming together to form a cohesive party to fight Home Rule. I know this from Bob, my younger brother. He has decided to resign and is willing to stand for election for Sinn Féin. We have set up a Sinn Féin group on our farm in Laragh. I have to say I've never been one to wait for some man to do it for me. I'll do it myself. I have since my girlhood in Glendalough House been reading

Arthur Griffith's *Sinn Féin* newspaper … now the name is being used to unite all nationalists, Catholic and Protestant … men and women … *well,* some women …

LOO: Is that not why we are here? Sinn Féin is no longer run by Arthur Griffith who had women central to the party. The new party are not including women the way they should.

CONSTANCE: Thank you *all.* Can we please start this meeting? Rosamond, can you read the minutes from our last meeting.

ROSAMOND: Our last meeting was held at Miss Barton's house. I propose a note of thanks be entered into the minute book for her kind gesture of meeting members at the station and motoring them to Glendalough House.

DULCIBELLA: As I am on intimate terms of friendship with the members of this group, I will permit a degree of familiarity, so you are permitted to call me Da, as these meetings are usually – today's excepted – held in the homes of our members.

MARY: It should be noted in the minute book that we are in the Ladies Room today, rather different from Glendalough House. Oh – I get the location now. Da's house was the first to have a flushing toilet in Wicklow! When we meet in ours I warn ye our convenience is outside *(giggling, laughter).*

CONSTANCE: Enough, I say! This is the most disorderly of our meetings to date! I know the location is a tad inconvenient, but it is important that we gather away from the eyes and ears of the men. It is becoming a critical situation – our roles which were assured with the leaders of the Rising are now not so. Despite the best efforts of those present – indeed all members of our group – all attempts have been made for our exclusion. Rosamond, please review, quickly, what the current situation is …

ROSAMOND: Dr Lynn, our sole representative, attended the meeting of the Council of Nine. She made us aware that this meeting of the Sinn Féin Executive was taking place and that we need to make sure that we are ready to select women for election when our time comes … to make sure we fight hard to have women represented on all Sinn Féin cumann.

CONSTANCE: Short and sweet, Rosamond. I know time is precious. Where is Dr Lynn? It is not like her not to be on time. When she is with us I will ask her to give a fuller update. She is meant to be chairing today, not me. Before that can I have someone to second these minutes.

EFFIE: I do!

CONSTANCE: Do it correctly, Effie. Say I second that! Hang on here, Effie, I was not aware that you were a member of the League of Women Delegates? You have to be selected by one of the respective groups of women to be here.

EFFIE: Mrs Ceannt said I could come and tell you she could not make it. Ummm … she gives her apologies … that's what she told me to say. You know that I work for her as a ladies maid … anyways, I have something I want to say to you, Madame Markievicz, and she said I would see you here. I told her it was mighty important and I wasn't sleeping … she said it was best to come see you today … I do want to talk to you …

CONSTANCE: In that case it can wait until what we call 'Any Other Business' at the end of the meeting.

The door opens with the sound of the swish of a long skirt and a hat being taken off.

KATHLEEN: My apologies, ladies (*breathlessly*). I got caught up with the meeting outside. I used the opportunity to give out the leaflet that Madeleine and I had printed with the money we made from selling the tricolour that was flown during the Rising and, of course, I got caught up in the discussion on the franchise!

CONSTANCE: Kathleen, time is passing. Can you fill us in on the Council of Nine.

KATHLEEN: Of course, as many of you know (*breathlessly*) I was proposed by this group to attend the Council of Nine chaired by Count Plunkett, when Josephine, his wife, was sick … she has not been right since Joe was executed.

MARY (*loud whisper*): I'm not surprised. I heard it might have been him – the one of the signatories who did not support the Proclamation being addressed to Irish men and Irish women!

CONSTANCE: Mary, Mary, Mary!

ROSAMOND (*interrupting*): Quite contrary.

DULCIBELLA: You should not be spreading vile gossip, Mary. It could have been someone else.

LOO: I heard it may have been Pearse who did not want it from the outset, but he was then convinced by Connolly. I have always personally suspected Éamonn Ceannt. I hate to verbalise it; upholding his memory is so important as we try to unite our people. But I knew him from Dolphin's Barn … he was our commander in the South Dublin Union … and Áine has said herself that she knew nothing of the Rising, even when the meetings were taking place in her house. What does that say for his trust in her? His value in the inclusion of women?

MARY: Well, it was not James Connolly, nor Thomas Mac Donagh – he was involved in the franchise movement – nor Tom Clarke, he used a worker, he did not care if they were men or women …

CONSTANCE: Mary, if you speak out of turn you must say 'through the chair' if you wish to speak. Otherwise you are not respecting the way the meeting is being conducted. Albeit even in these surroundings it is still a meeting nonetheless.

KATHLEEN: Before I continue I must implore you to stop all this talk behind the back of our dear friend Áine – one of our closest colleagues. A secret oath-bound society is just that. All I know is that this is destructive and dividing talk. It is not for us to speculate. It was done in secret. We will never know who it was ... but does it *really* matter? Whomsoever it was he did sign it ... so isn't that enough? By signing the Proclamation they, all seven, stated they believed in equal citizenship.

CONSTANCE: Please, ladies, this is not helping our cause. I understand that there is some difficulty around the makeup of this group. Please continue, Kathleen, explain for the members who do not know what has happened.

KATHLEEN: Well ... to give him credit Count Plunkett took the step of bringing people together. You will remember he was sent to an open prison in England.

MARY (*talking to Loo*): He went to Oxford. He wanted to read in the library there, but I understand that he was not admitted as one of the librarians did not approve of the Rising. I was not out so quick neither – refused to say I wouldn't do it again.

Laughter.

CONSTANCE: Can I have some order! These surroundings do not lend themselves to composure. Please delegates, pay attention. Mary, I am going to get another delegate from the Women Workers' Union if you keep talking out of turn. Loo, I am surprised at you, allowing her to go on with these transgressions. Please continue, Kathleen.

KATHLEEN: Count Plunkett selected his wife ...

MARY: Or she selected herself!

CONSTANCE: Mary, please desist, or I will be obliged to exclude you.

KATHLEEN: Countess Plunkett was ill, and I was able to take her place at the group's meeting. Suffice to say, things are moving at a rapid rate. Male differences are being smoothed over and they are managing this without any consultation with women.

ROSAMOND: They don't see the need to consult us.

KATHLEEN: They don't see things like the men who addressed us in their manifesto at Easter 1916 – Irishmen and Irishwomen. Equal rights and equal opportunities are gone, ladies. It is a fight to keep our place at that table … or any table. The Council of Nine have decided to expand it to include the returning prisoners … but do I need to add that this new expanded council, this group will *not* have an extra space for women; our one seat has now gone. We complained that the one seat was the seat for a man's wife … now it has become no seat for women … the removal of a token woman!

CONSTANCE: I understand that the plan for this amalgamation was mooted when Countess Plunkett, the sole woman, was on the council and she did not see fit to tell us, the women of Ireland, that we have been banished from the political organisation which is going to fight for Irish independence? Can you tell us, Alice, what is the update on your husband Laurence's position and what do you know of events for members of parliament in London?

ALICE: Thank you, Con. I am not here as a token woman or because I am the wife of a politician. Firstly, let me say to those of you who don't know, Laurence and I have moved to Dublin. We have made our sacrifice. Sold our home at a loss (*sigh*) to give ourselves to the Irish cause. We have equally shared an interest in politics. I have worked as his secretary for many years. I do disagree when people talk about women being outside politics. Laurence has left the Irish Parliamentary Party for eight years now and has, as you know, been an Independent, serving in Westminster. The leader of the Irish Parliamentary Party, John Redmond, does not want to have anything to do with the franchise question until there is Home Rule. That is immaterial to Laurence now; he is giving his allegiance to Sinn Féin, the organisation under which all nationalists are gathering, and he will, if elected, undertake a policy of abstentionism and stay away from Westminster. He is with us and he will do everything to let women have an equal part to play in politics. I assure you I would not have married him if I had not thought we would have equality in all things. Laurence is a good man. But I am not here to speak for him; I speak for myself. If we are excluded from meetings it is important that we have news of what happens inside closed doors.

LOO: Closed doors! Ever since Mary closed that door, we have discussed nothing, and I mean nothing of substance! Madame Markievicz, we do not have time to digress into conversation, this is a meeting. Can I have my say?

CONSTANCE: Dr Lynn is now in the chair.

KATHLEEN: You can go ahead, Loo. Say what you have to say, if Mrs Ginnell is finished.

ALICE: Yes, I am.

LOO: I know what the new group is being called; it is to be called the Sinn Féin Executive Committee. It may be Sinn Féin in name – the name coined by Máire Butler if I remember correctly – but it is not like that organisation that was formed with men and women by Arthur Griffith in 1905. It is using that name ... and some of the policies ... but by God not the equality ...

The sound of a tap running – of someone washing their hands.

EFFIE: Sorry, Madame, my hands were grubby after coming on the tram. You can never be sure when you touch a stranger if they will give you a sickness.

CONSTANCE: Desist from using the facilities of this place until we are finished.

ROSAMOND: If I may, chair, I wish to present to the group the list of names of women who have agreed to represent us in various departments – agriculture, education, poor law, health. We have found willing and able women who will work in these areas, including Dr Lynn.

KATHLEEN: Yes, I wish to focus on matters of health and the well-being of mothers and children. Children are dying all around us – there are those in this room who have lost babies. It is time to make our feelings into actions. You are probably aware that I have been talking with Madeleine – Miss ffrench-Mullen. We want to set up our own hospital. It is so necessary that we women look after women and see if we can stop the deaths of so many children. More children die in Dublin than the streets of Calcutta in India with its streets teeming with the poor. Sorry now I am doing it and I am chairing. Honestly I do believe this setting is not conducive to a proper meeting! *(Laughter).*

ROSAMOND: May I continue then. I have got names of some women countrywide from Cumann na mBan. Many have experience in teaching, farming, nursing and one or two have been Poor Law Guardians. They are willing to play their part in the making of laws and governing ...

CONSTANCE: We need to focus on practical actions, logical steps or otherwise we are doomed. We will never get an active part in government. We will not be allowed to rule, to make laws for ourselves. Women have from till very recently stood so far removed from all politics that we need to formulate a much clearer and more incisive view of the political situation than men.

ROSAMOND: One of the steps we have taken is to write Dr Dillon, Count and Countess Plunkett's son-in-law. He is sympathic to our actions. We asked him to point out that women are equally eligible with men to be delegates for councils. It is hoped that there would be a fair percentage of women elected when we get a chance to fight an election.

DULCIBELLA: Can I get us to reflect on why we are gathered here, in the Mansion House's ladies lavatory, God help us! My worry is that we are dealing with new men. All the members of the Provisional Committee of the Irish Republic are gone, dead. The only surviving leader is Eamon de Valera and even then he was not a member of the Provisional Government of the Irish Republic. He was never a member of the Irish Republican Brotherhood as far as I know ... We have no idea what he is going to do ... We cannot trust any man. We cannot let anyone know of what we are thinking, so we can have the advantage of surprise. I have no intention of telling Bob anything but what I want him to know. Alice, I would be very judicious in what you share with Laurence.

ALICE: I do not want to be personal, Miss Barton, but as you have never had a husband I would ask you to respect me and what I want to discuss with my husband is my personal business.

KATHLEEN (*gently and quietly*): Alice, I too have no husband, nor has, as you have pointed out, Dulcibella, Loo or Rosamond. Indeed Con is the only one who has one, and Casi has been away for almost a decade fighting for his own country. So I have to echo what

Dulcibella has said – you alone are the one who has to be judicious in your dealings. We can have no leaks from this group. What is being said here about new leaders is after all personal opinion based on very little knowledge. What if Eamon de Valera is young, we have no idea how all this adulation will go to his head. I worry that he will not be up to the job, and that he will not value the role of women …

LOO: Not so young! Sure he is must be middle-aged – at least 35!

KATHLEEN (*laughs*): Young to us, Loo!

MARY: By the chair … don't you forget that he did not accept women in his garrison!

LOO: I heard that men serving with him said that he was soon regretting that as he had no women to cook or do first aid and that meant that his men had to do soldiering …

CONSTANCE: General Maxwell did not see the role the women played, releasing nearly every woman, but these men do. Remember I was not held with the men in prison; I have not got into the inner circle. They were all together in internment camps and jails. Plotting and scheming, as you always say, Mary, on how they would start a call for independence, to take over power. They have their leaders selected, the champions are already in place. Look at Michael Collins – he is the one to watch.

DULCIBELLA: Yes, he is a brainy one. Kathleen Clarke thinks he is so like Seán Mac Diarmada, a charmer, a good man. Mrs Clarke is putting her trust in him. She has given him access to all our contacts of the families who receive aid. I'm not sure I trust him to do the job. That sort of man I never … ever trust. All sliding up to you, arm around the shoulder stuff. Mick Collins goes on with that same sort of ould guff while ye all swoon.

But he is to head up the spy network and he *does* need our help.

LOO: Miss Barton, that's our problem, we see ourselves, as helpers, enablers. What did Máire Colum write about Cumann na mBan before the Rising? 'We are not the handmaidens or the camp followers of the Volunteers!' Now look at us. Let's not let Cumann na mBan continue that role. I did not join the organisation for that reason. I did not approve of raising money for the Defence of Ireland Fund ... for buying a gun for an individual Volunteer! I heard Sorcha McDermott came from London with the sole purpose of handing her gun to Tom Clarke, the fruit of her fundraising! Why did she not keep it for herself?

ALICE: The rank and file of Cumann na mBan should not be subjected to ridicule or diminished for their actions – they are only as good as their leaders. I know from my branch in London. We have to recruit, we have a rallying cry to continue what was started last year. Our organisation was fledging when the Rising happened. We will now show what the women can do. As delegates we must lead ...

CONSTANCE: Lead ladies! The reason for this meeting is we are being *ignored*. The amalgamation of the Sinn Féin and Liberty Club has happened. Members of the Irish Volunteers are automatically being included, but Cumann na mBan, the female counterpart of that organisation, has not had *their* representatives co-opted.

ROSAMOND: Yes, Madame, some of Cumann na mBan seem to glory in death and distruction, the excitement of it all, of war ... some of them don't even understand politics as they think it is men's business. They don't see we have a role.

MARY: It is unbelievable! Whoops, sorry, chair! After we fought alongside them! I suppose the writing was on the wall the way some of the senior members of Cumann na mBan were treated during the Rising. Waiting for orders that never came … while we in the Irish Citizen Army marched alongside the men …

ALICE: How can we make our voices heard? Recruit strong women who won't be ignored?

ROSAMOND: I will record our surprise and indignation of this action in our minute book.

KATHLEEN: Noting our reaction for posterity will do nothing, Miss Jacob. We can't accept this, and we must change it.

CONSTANCE: Kathleen, it is about making our voices count. We need for the women of the future to know the truth of these events. Rosamond, I hope you made note of the location of this meeting – the historians of the future will be interested in that! We need to get out to stand our ground and make our case for the young women of the future. And with that I will conclude this meeting …

EFFIE: Excuse me, Madame, I want to do that business thing … (*sighing*) … I need to leave.

ROSAMOND (*interrupting*): We all do! The meeting is about to start in the Round Room. Hundreds of organisations with a handful of women.

EFFIE: No, I mean leave you … um … the movement … the fight. What I am saying is I have done my bit now and I am going to be married and my Jimmy does not want me to be … caught up with youse all anymore. I have to give it up or else he won't marry me!

CONSTANCE: Effie, I am surprised, shocked actually, you would even think of leaving the movement? You have been with us since those days in Liberty Hall, in the soup kitchens making food for the strikers, out in the Rising and for the past year one of the best workers in the field, distributing money to the families of prisoners.

I heard all about your involvement when I got out of prison. What sort of a hold does this man have on you? Surely you learned from all of us that you have your own mind? You are your own independent person. You can't get married to a man who won't let you be.

EFFIE: I wasn't sure when he first said it, so I went to speak to Fr Molloy, our parish priest who will marry us. I told him all I had done ... and that Jimmy wants us to settle down and not to be gallivanting anymore. Fr Molloy told me to listen to my fiancé, he will be my husband and I will have to obey him when I am a married woman. He gave me the *Catholic Messenger* about the duties of a Catholic girl to her home and family and how it is important to focus on babbies and not to be distracted by the evils. Women having their own money corrupts the morals of a woman put on the earth to be a mother, it does. A distraction from our God-given role in life.

CONSTANCE: I have recently converted to become a Catholic but that doctrine will control you, destroy you, Effie. James Connolly called the Irish woman 'the slave of the slave'. Effie, don't be blinded by love. You will be a prisoner in that marriage ...

EFFIE (*starts to sob*): That's what they said ... they said you, Madame, would work on my mind. Fr Molloy and my Jimmy both said that you women would play on my mind and overpower me. Fr Molloy said you were a corruptor of women, whose husband ran off and who did not have her child. You gave your own daughter to your mother far away so you could run wild ...

MARY AND ALICE: Effie, stop! Stop at once!

ROSAMOND: Effie, you're speaking out of turn.

DULCIBELLA: Oh! Do not speak to your elder, your superior, in that manner!

EFFIE (*shouting*): I know my place! You're always acting as my friend, but you're not. I speak the truth! (*Places her hands over her ears*). You're spinsters, barren women. I want lots of children and the love of a man. Loving Ireland won't give you nothing! You'll get nothing! I must do what me church and me fella wants. They told me you'd try and bewitch me. Please let me go … Let me out … I must leave …

The door opens and closes with a bang. Loud knocking on the door.

MALE ATTENDANT: Is everything all right in there?

Taps running. The sound of rustling of clothes and hats. The sound of makeup being applied.

ALICE: Yes, yes, it is, young man, thank you. We are just powdering our noses.

CONSTANCE: Let me open the door. After my time in prison you have no idea the joy of opening and closing doors! Ladies, it is time to leave the lavatory.

THE END

BIBLIOGRAPHY

Key Sources:

Hanna Sheehy Skeffington Papers, the National Library of Ireland, MS 21,194 (47) Minute Book of the Women Delegates to the All Ireland Conference (Cumann na Teachtaire).

Margaret Ward 'The League of Women Delegates and Sinn Féin', *History Ireland,* Volume 4, Issue 3, Autumn 1996.

Additional Source Material:

Genealogy.ie

Census 1901 and 1911, National Archives of Ireland.

DULCIBELLA BARTON

Dulcibella Barton, Bureau of Military History Witness Statement #936 [*author's note: there are some factual errors in this statement. Please see Barton Family Tree by Charlene Newport on Geni.com. This was cross referenced with certification on genealogy.ie*].

Martin Timmons, 'Part Four – Wicklow Eyewitness Accounts: 'Da' Barton's Account in Wicklow and the 1916 Rising', *Roundwood and District Historical and Folklore Society Journal,* No. 11, 2016.

Rory W. Childers, 'Glendalough House and Derralossary: A Memoir', *Roundwood and District Historical and Folklore Society Journal,* No. 11, 2000.

ALICE GINNELL

Alice Ginnell, Bureau of Military History Witness Statement #982.

MARY PEROLZ

Máire Perolz (Mrs Flanagan) Bureau of Military History Witness Statement #246.

MARGARET 'LOO' KENNEDY

Margaret 'Loo' Kennedy, Military Archives Pension
Record WMSP34REF596.

ROSAMOND JACOB

Leeann Lane, *Rosamond Jacob: Third Person Singular*
(University College Dublin Press, 2010).

DR KATHLEEN LYNN

Margaret Ó hÓgartaigh, *Kathleen Lynn: Irishwoman, Patriot,
Doctor* (Irish Academic Press, 2006).

CONSTANCE DE MARKIEVICZ

Anne Haverty, *Constance Markievicz: Irish Revolutionary*
(Lilliput Press, 2016).

Anne Marreco, *The Rebel Countess: The Life and Times of
Constance Markievicz* (Weidenfeld & Nicolson, 1967).

Jacqueline Van Voris, *Constance de Markievicz in the Cause of
Ireland* (University of Massachusetts Press, 1967).

Joe McGowan, *Constance Markievicz: The People's Countess*
(Sligo, 2003).

ACKNOWLEDGEMENTS

Firstly, I wish to thank Alan Hayes, publisher of Arlen House, the oldest and largest feminist press in Ireland; without his dedication to and appreciation of women of the past our documenting of Irish women's contributions in the present would be far less informed and nuanced. Thank you for publishing my first play.

I am also extremely grateful to Gráinne Blair for reading early drafts and encouraging me to continue with this new departure. Thank you also to Paul Turnell who, as always, has assisted me with my research – two minds have always been better than one! Thank you also to Maggie Mulhare for her support and encouragement in all things creative.

Thank you to my husband Eamon for his continuing support of my work; the title was his suggestion. Thank you also to Eve and Edward for encouraging me to write something new.

I was assisted with information which facilitated the dramatisation of some of the characters in this play. Thank you especially to Elinor and John Medlycott for supplying me with copies of articles on the Barton family taken from the *Roundwood and District Historical and Folklore Society Journal*. Thank you for Erskine C. Childers for use of the image of Dulcibella and her puppy Wicklow, 1909, which is taken from the Erskine C. Childers Collection.

Thank you to Leeann Lane for use of the image of Rosamond Jacob dating to 1912 when she was 24; as her biographer I hope you will be happy in how I have depicted her in this play.

Thank you to Ed Penrose for his help as always. I am grateful to the Irish Labour History Society for permission to use Lily Williams' image of Dr Kathleen Lynn (1919) on the back cover of the book.

Thank you to the staff of the Military Archives, in particular to Hugh Beckett for his assistance. The image of Mary Perolz is courtesy of the Military Archives. It is taken from a photograph of members of the Irish Citizen Army gathered outside the ruined Liberty Hall, Easter 1917 [IE-MA-BMH-CD-119-3-5]. The image of Alice Ginnell is a detail from a group photograph taken at the conferring of the freedom of the city on Constance de Markievicz, 17 July 1917, and is reproduced here courtesy of the Military Archives. The unidentified press cutting of Margaret Loo Kennedy is also courtesy of the Military Archives, taken from her Pension Record [MSP34REF596].

Thank you to Aoife Torpey of Kilmainham Gaol Museum, who has been unfailingly good natured and speedy in response to my queries as I searched for images that I have a vague memory of seeing twenty years ago during my time working in Kilmainham Gaol. The image of Constance Markievicz and Poppet is a detail from a picture taken in Waterford in 1917 [18PO-1A21-18]. The image of Dr Lynn [21PO-IA21-19] which was given to Brigid Davis, Christmas 1936, is also courtesy of Kilmainham Gaol Museum.

Thank you to the O'Brien Collection for the use of the Lily Williams painting 'Hibernia' 1916. I am very grateful to Curator Marty Fahey for his generous support and interest in this publication.

The first reading of *Leaving the Ladies* is by Smashing Times Film and Theatre Company. Thank you to Mary Moynihan, Freda Manweiler and Niamh Clowry. I am delighted to be working with Mary Moynihan, Smashing Times CEO and director of the first rehearsed reading of this play at the National Library of Ireland on 26 September 2019 as part of the Dublin Arts and Human Rights Festival.

The first reading of *Leaving the Ladies* is produced by Smashing Times and directed by Mary Moynihan in the National Library of Ireland on 26 September 2019.

Smashing Times is a professional theatre and film company involved in performance, training and participation. It was established in 1991 by a group of women actors who met at the Focus Theatre, Dublin. Today the work takes place at local, national, and international levels in a range of settings – on screen, on stage from the professional arts and theatre space to local schools and communities where we are invited to work with people collaboratively, and at European and international levels. The work of the company is underpinned by a rights-based approach and a commitment to artistic excellence and social engagement.

As a leading professional arts organisation the company develops cutting edge projects that promote social justice, peace, gender equality, human rights, positive mental health, anti-racism, and more through high quality artistic processes, merging art, culture and politics to interact and engage with contemporary society and the world we live in.

Smashing Times have launched a world-class international Smashing Times Online Centre for the Arts and Equality which is a key resource service and networking forum providing information, training and a platform for discussion on using the arts to promote and protect gender equality and human rights. This online centre is kindly funded by the Arts and Culture Capital Scheme, Department of Culture, Heritage and the Gaeltacht.

LILY WILLIAMS (1874–1940)

Elizabeth Josephine Williams (known as Lily), came from a large Dublin family. Lily was first taught by Mary Manning who was a formative influence on many young women artists. She later attended the Metropolitan School of Art. In 1903 she first exhibited with the Young Irish Artists and was reported in the press as having a skill in feminine portraits in watercolour and that she was 'clever in poses and expression'. In 1909 when the third Young Irish Artists exhibition took place in Leinster Hall on Molesworth Street, her art college contemporaries Mary Swanzy and Estella Solomons also contributed, along with Willie Pearse (brother of P.H. Pearse), Grace Gifford and William Leech.

By 1911 Lily was active in the Celtic revival; she is recorded, along with her sisters Norah and Flo, as speaking both Irish and English. She was a member of the Irish Guild of the Church (Cumann Gaelach na hEaglais) which sought an Irish language version of the Church of Ireland liturgy.

The Williams family members who lived in 11 Lower Beechwood Avenue, Ranelagh were politically supportive of the 1916 Rising and the campaign for independence which followed. Lily had her own studio on Pembroke Street (where on at least one occasion Eamon de Valera hid).

Many of her paintings were of friends; she painted two portraits of Dr Kathleen Lynn, one of which is in the Royal College of Physicians of Ireland and the other is in the Irish Labour History Society. She contributed to *The Book of St Ultan*, which was a fundraiser for the Children's Hospital which had been set up Dr Kathleen Lynn in 1919. Lily was elected an Associate of the Royal Hibernian Academy in 1929. In 1933 she contributed to an Irish exhibition in Chicago. In 1944 there was a posthumous Grafton Academy exhibition of her work which included a portrait of The O'Rahilly who had been killed during the 1916 Rising.

Over the past number of years John and Patricia O'Brien have formed The O'Brien Collection. They have brought together unique pieces of fine art, decorative arts, antiques, artefacts and furniture, dating from the eighteenth century to the present. The Collection reflects the family's journey as emigrants from Ireland in the late nineteenth century to Chicago, a city with a wealth of Irish culture and heritage.

The Collection is built around core events which have had an impact on Irish people – the famine, the land wars and nationalism of the late nineteenth and early twentieth centuries, with a key focus on the Easter Rising; in each case an item is selected for the Collection according to Curator Marty Fahey 'that expresses and celebrates the breadth, depth and beauty of Irish artistic creativity and material culture'.

The Collection contains works by Aloysius O'Kelly, Walter Osbourne, Paul Henry, Jack Yeats, Harry Clarke, Mildred Ann Butler, William Leech, William Orpen, John Lavery, Mainie Jellett, Mary Swanzy, Sean Keating, Charles Lamb, Sean O'Sullivan and contemporary artists including Robert Ballagh, John Behan, Rowan Gillespie, James Hanley and Colin Davidson.

Among the material culture that is collected alongside this impressive list of Irish artists, past and present, are flags (William Halpin's own tricolour), banners, folk items include a penal cross from Lough Derg in Donegal dating to 1725, and musical instruments such as a harpsichord made in 1798 by William Southwell in Dublin and a John Egan harp used at the time of Robert Emmet's rebellion in 1801. Modern items include a tapestry by Louis le Brocquy dating to the 1950s to contemporary pieces by furniture designer Joseph Walsh of Cork.

According to the Curator, Marty Fahey, himself a musician: 'Key to the intentionality of the Collection, is, further, a desire to foster opportunities for exhibitions around these themes and to inspire creative responses and collaborations with other colleagues (*artists, musicians, poets, writers, historians, curators and other scholars*) who share similar interests and passions'.

Items from the Collection have been lent to exhibitions both in Ireland and in the US. In 2015 one such exhibition was 'Ireland: Crossroads of Art and Design 1690–1840' (see Aileen Dillane, 'Crossroads of Art and Design: musically curating and mediating Irish cultural artefacts in Chicago' *Éire-Ireland*, 54:1&2 Spring/Summer 2019).

For more information, please contact Marty Fahey (Curator) at marty.fahey@obrienintl.net

Dr Sinéad McCoole has written extensively on modern Irish history, specialising in the role of women. Her books include *Hazel: A Life of Lady Lavery* (1996); *Guns and Chiffon* (1997); *No Ordinary Women* (2003); *Easter Widows* (2014) and *Mná* (2018). She has over three decades experience as a practitioner in the area of public history, focusing on Irish culture, arts and history. As a museum curator she has brought academic research to life for the public through the selection and presentation of documents, artefacts and costumes. An accomplished scriptwriter, her films include *Women of 1916* (1997) and *Guns and Chiffon* (2003).

She curated *Mná 1916*, the national centenary exhibition on the role of women, which toured venues throughout Ireland, as well as being presented by Irish embassies and missions internationally. *Crossings* (2011), part of the Imagine Ireland showcase in the US, and *Drawing Conclusions: Mapping the Irish* (2012) were both held in the American Irish Historical Society, New York City.

A member of the Irish Government's Expert Advisory Group on the Decade of Commemorations, she was Curatorial and Historical Advisor to the Ireland 2016 Centenary Programme and in 2018 was an Ex-Officio member of *Vótáil100*. She is currently curating an exhibition to commemorate the centenary of Irish women in politics and public life as part of the Commemorations Unit of the Department of Culture, Heritage and the Gaeltacht.

Leaving the Ladies is her first play.